Late Settings

BOOKS BY JAMES MERRILL

Poetry

Fiction

Late Settings

Poems by

James Merrill

Atheneum · New York · 1985

Most of these poems have appeared in the following magazines:

THE ATLANTIC MONTHLY *(Santo)*
THE GEORGIA REVIEW *(Think Tank, Page from the Koran)*
GRAND STREET *(Bronze)*
HORIZON *(Channel 13)*
THE KENYON REVIEW *(Caesarion)*
THE MASSACHUSETTS REVIEW *(Last Mornings in California)*
THE NATION *(Lenses)*
THE NEW YORKER *(Clearing the Title, The Pier: Under Pisces, Palm Beach with
    Portuguese Man-of-War, Revivals of* Tristan, *The "Metro", An Upset,
    Peter's Tattoos, A Day on the Connecticut River, Santorini: Stopping the
    Leak)*
THE NEW YORK REVIEW OF BOOKS *(The School Play, The House Fly, Month,
    Casual Wear, Popular Demand, Valéry: Palme)*
THE PARIS REVIEW *(Grass, Island in the Works, Domino, In the Dark)*
PLOUGHSHARES *(Ideas, Trees Listening to Bach)*
POETRY *(The Blue Grotto, After the Ball)*
RARITAN *(Arclight, Radiometer)*
SHENANDOAH *(The Help)*
VERSE *(Midsummer Evening on the Prinsengracht)*
THE YALE REVIEW *(Developers at Crystal River, Days of 1941 and '44)*

Published simultaneously in Canada by Collier Macmillan Canada, Inc.
ISBN 0-689-11572-5 (cloth); 0-689-11579-2 (paper)
Library of Congress catalog card number 84-45706
Composition by P & M Typesetting, Inc., Waterbury, Connecticut
*Manufactured by Halliday Lithograph Corporation, West Hanover and
Plympton, Massachusetts*
Designed by Harry Ford
First printing April 1985
Second printing October 1985

*For my sister Doris
and my brother Charles*

CONTENTS

I

GRASS

The river irises
Draw themselves in.
Enough to have seen
Their day. The arras

Also of evening drawn,
We light up between
Earth and Venus
On the courthouse lawn,

Kept by this cheerful
Inch of green
And ten more years—fifteen?—
From disappearing.

CLEARING THE TITLE

for DJ

Because the wind has changed, because I guess
My poem (what to call it though?) is finished,
Because the golden genie chafes within
His smudged-glass bottle and, god help us, you
Have chosen, sight unseen, this tropic rendezvous
Where tourist, outcast and in-groupie gather
Island by island, linked together,
Causeways bridging the vast shallowness—

Through the low ceiling motors rip.
Below me, twisting in the asphalt grip
Of mall and pancake house, boatel and bank,
What's left of Nature here? Those trees five thousand tin
Roofs, like little mirrors in distress,
Would flash up from if the sun were out . . .
Oh for the lucid icebound book of winter
I gave up my rapt place in for this trip!

Such a mistake—past fifty and behaving
As if hope sprang eternal. At the baggage claim
Armed with *The Power and the Glory* (Greene),
I notice, finger-drawn in a soaped pane,
One black sun only, spokes in air
Like legs of a big bug flipped on its back,
Above a clumsy WELLCOME TO THE KEYS
—Then see the open car. You in it, waving.

Couldn't one have gone into the matter
Before succumbing? Easier said than done,
What with this tough white coral skeleton
Beneath a crop of shanties built on blocks,
On air, on edge for, any day,
Water and wind to sweep them clean away—
Ill-braced like me, capricious chatterbox,
Against your blasts of horn and floods of casual patter.

4

Sales patter? The appalling truth now bores
Into my brain: you've *bought* a house
And pass, en route to it, the peeling white
Five-story skyscraper in which "our" title
Is being cleared!—activity no more
Thinkable (you park, fling a green-painted door
Open onto a fresh white hall)
Than what the termites do, look! to these floors

Between the muddy varnish of whose lines
(But can you picture *living* here? Expect
Me to swelter, year by sunset year,
Beneath these ceilings?—which at least aren't low.
What about houses elsewhere, rooms already packed
With memories? That chiffonier
Would have to go, or else be painted white . . .)
More brightly with each word the daylight shines.

And fresh as paint the bare rooms, if you please,
Having consumed whatever came before,
Look up unblinking: will *we* bring
Their next meal—table, mirror, bed, lamp, chair?
Serve the ravenous interior
With real-life victuals, voices, vanities
Until it lolls back purring?—like our slum
Garden zonked by milk-bombs from two old bent trees.

Presuming, then, tripod and pendulum
Tell truly, and the freckled county clerk
Completes, adds to the master file
A Gothic-lettered "title" with your name—
What happens next? Behind a latticework
Of deeds no one has time or patience to undo
We cultivate our little lot, meanwhile
Waiting companionably for kingdom come?

Clearing the Title

Close-ups: hibiscus broad as garden hats.
Large winged but nameless insect excavated
By slaves; the abdomen's deep strata
Primitive-intricate, like macramé.
Then from beneath the house, fee fi fo fum!
Caller the color of good smoke blown through the years
Into this dumb scarred mug he lifts to say:
"Huh? Not want *me*? Man, the whole world wants *cats*!"

No. No, no, no. We can't just cast
Three decades' friendships and possessions out.
Who're our friends here? (In fact I recognize
Old ones everywhere I turn my eyes—
Trumpet-vine, cracked pavement, that faint sulphur smell,
Those see-through lizards, quick as a heartbeat . . .)
But people? (Well, the Wilburs live downstreet . . .)
Of course, if shutting doors onto the past

Could damage *it* . . . Wherever that thought led,
Turning the loose knob onto better-late-
Than-never light, we breast its deepening stream
Along with others who've a date
With sunset. Each day's unspent zinc or red brass penny
—Here at land's end not deposited
In winter palisades crowned by antennae,
Fuel for the all-night talk shows of the dead—

Inflates to moidore, melts toward an oblivion
Alone, its gravity unspecified,
The far-off mangrove islet saves
From being wholly formed of air and waves,
Of light and birdcry, as with each step less
Divides the passer-through from, what to call
Such radiance—creative? terminal?
Day's flush of pleasure, knowing its poem done?

Our poem now. It's signed JM, but grew
From life together, grain by coral grain.
Building on it, we let the life cloud over . . .
Time to break through those clouds, for heaven's sake,
And look round. Any place will do
(Remember, later at the discothèque)
And what at first appall precisely are the changes
That everybody is entitled to.

Here at the end's a landing stage swept clean
Of surplus "properties" and "characters".
Gone the thick banyan, the opaque old queen.
Only some flimsiest human veil
Woven of trickster and revivalist,
Musician and snake-charmer (and, yes, us as well)
Pot- and patchouli-scented floats between
The immense warm pink spotlight and the scene.

Here's the Iguana Man, from lands
"Beneath the world". Dragons, withered like him,
Unwinking drape his fishnet singlet. Here
Balloons are straining for release; we pick
A headstrong silver one. And here a clown
Cat-limber, white-lipped with a bright cerulean tear
On one rouged cheek, rides unicycle, hands
Nonchalantly juggling firebrands.

Circles round every act form, or to groans
Disperse. This portion of the dock's been cleared
By the Salvation Army. (They're
Nine strong, a family; beneath the same
Grim visor glowers, babe to grandmother,
The same grim love.) "Y'all give!" our deadpan clown
Yells brandishing a hammer fit for Thor,
"Give or Ah'll clobber yew!" and *grunt* go the trombones.

Though no one does, no thunder strikes. Because—
Say, because a black girl with shaved skull
Sways on the brink: flexed knee and ankle-bell
And eyes that burn back at the fiery ball
Till it relenting tests with one big toe
Its bath, and Archimedean splendors overflow.
As the sun sets, "Let's hear it for the sun!"
Cry voices. Laughter. Bells. Applause

(Think of the dead here, sleeping above ground
—Simpler than to hack a tomb from coral—
In whitewashed hope chests under the palm fronds.
Or think of waking, whether to the quarrel
Of white cat and black crow, those unchanged friends,
Or to a dazzle from below:
Earth visible through floor-cracks, miles—or inches—down,
And spun by a gold key-chain round and round . . .)

Whereupon on high, where all is bright
Day still, blue turning to key lime, to steel
A clear flame-dusted crimson bars,
Sky puts on the face of the young clown
As the balloons, mere hueless dots now, stars
Or periods—although tonight we trust no real
Conclusions will be reached—float higher yet,
Juggled slowly by the changing light.

ISLAND IN THE WORKS

From air seen fathom-deep
But rising to a head—
Abscess of the abyss
Any old night letting rip
Its fires, yearlong,
As roundabout waves hiss—

Jaded by untold blue
Subversions, watered-down
Moray and Spaniard . . .
Now to construe
In the original
Those at first arid, hard,

Soon rootfast, ramifying,
Always more fruitful
Dialogues with light.
Various dimwit under-
graduate types will wonder
At my calm height,

Vapors by then surmounted
(Merely another phase?)
And how in time I trick
Out my new "shores" and "bays"
With small craft, shrimpers'
Bars and rhetoric.

Darkly the Old Ones grumble
I'll hate all that. Hate words,
Their schooling flame?
The spice grove chatted up
By small gray knowing birds?
Myself given a name?

Island in the Works

Waves, as your besetting
Depth-wish recedes,
I'm surfacing, I'm home!
Open the atlas. Here:
This dot, securely netted
Under the starry dome.

(Unlike this page—no sooner
Brought to the pool than wafted
Out of reach, laid flat
Face-up on cool glares, ever
So lightly swayed, or swaying . . .
Now who did that?)

DEVELOPERS AT CRYSTAL RIVER

Elysian glade—
Roilings, upshudderings
Of tinsel, mirror-sycamores in wind . . .
No, we are underwater.
These are the Springs:
From deep below the bottom of white sand
Mercurial baubles effervesce
To aerate
A glassed-in bower of bliss
They keep at 74 degrees.

The mother manatees,
Brought here as babies, bring their babies here
To see the year-round decorations
And revel in each "tree's"
Renewing fruitlessness.
Muses of sheer
Indolence they are, and foes
To nothing in creation
—Least of all, those
Luscious undulating lawns downstream

Plowing through which, a sudden
Tenor scream,
The power launch veers—on guard!
Paths widen blue, then redden . . .
The huge, myopic cows go unheard. Poor
Finely-wrinkled humps
Over and over scarred
By the propellers, gaffs and garden tools
The boatmen use on them for fun,
Each year are fewer.

Developers at Crystal River

Sweet heaven, here comes one—
No heavier than a sigh
Or small dirigible
Gone limp, or adipose
Naiad walking through murk, on knives. Unmarriageable
(Unless to the Prince of Whales)
In her backwater court
She'll have escaped our human hells—?
Look how the blades have cut
Even into her.

Intuiting the visitor,
She drifts closer;
Flippers held out, deprecative but lonely,
Makes to salute
Her long-lost cousin with *his*
Flippers, his camera and visor.
Time stops as, face to face,
She offers what he'll only
Back on Earth find words for—a rueful, chaste,
Unshaven kiss.

THINK TANK

Because our young were drab
And slow to grow, for Carnival we ate them,
Pennants of motley distancing the deed
In the dechlorinated crystal slab.

The harlequin all grace and greed
Made glancing mincemeat of the mirror kissed.
The scholar blotched with ich
Sank into lonely shudderings.

But at our best we were of one mind,
Did our own sick or vital things
Within a medium secured by trick

Reflections over which, day, night, the braille
Eraser glided of the Snail
Our servant, huge and blind.

THE PIER: UNDER PISCES

The shallows, brighter,
Wetter than water,
Tepidly glitter with the fingerprint-
Obliterating feel of kerosene.

Each piling like a totem
Rises from rock bottom
Straight through the ceiling
Aswirl with suns, clear ones or pale bluegreen,

And beyond! where bubbles burst,
Sphere of their worst dreams,
If dream is what they do,
These floozy fish—

Ceramic-lipped in filmy
Peekaboo blouses,
Fluorescent body
Stockings, hot stripes,

Swayed by the hypnotic ebb and flow
Of supermarket Muzak,
Bolero beat the undertow's
Pebble-filled gourds repeat;

Jailbait consumers of subliminal
Hints dropped from on high
In gobbets none
Eschews as minced kin;

Who, hooked themselves—bamboo diviner
Bent their way
Vigorously nodding
Encouragement—

Are one by one hauled kisswise, oh
Into some blinding hell
Policed by leathery ex-
Justices each

Minding his catch, if catch is what he can,
If mind is what one means—
The torn mouth
Stifled by newsprint, working still. If . . . if . . .

The little scales
Grow stiff. Dusk plugs her dryer in,
Buffs her nails, riffles through magazines,
While far and wide and deep

Rove the great sharkskin-suited criminals
And safe in this lit shrine
A boy sits. He'll be eight.
We've drunk our milk, we've eaten our stringbeans,

But left untasted on the plate
The fish. An eye, a broiled pearl, meeting mine,
I lift his fork . . .
The bite. The tug of fate.

THE HELP

Louis Leroy, gentleman's gentleman
Among cashmeres and shantungs never quite
Caught smoking; shiftless Beulah with her fan,
Easing her dream books out of sight;
Jules all morning sharpening the bright
Kitchen knives, his one dull eye on Grace . . .
—The whole arranged so that *we* might,
Seeing nothing, say they Knew Their Place.

Gods they lived by, like the Numbers Man
Supremely dapper in the back porchlight,
Their very skins, cocoa and tan
Up the scale to glistening anthracite,
Challenged yet somehow smiled away the white
Small boy on Emma's lap: home base
Of common scents. Starch, sweat, snuff, they excite
Me still. Her arms round me, I knew my place.

James Madison, who chauffeured the sedan . . .
Shirt off in the garage after a fight
"At my friend's house," red streamers ran
Down his tall person, filling me with fright
—Or had I gained an abrupt, gasping height
Viewed from which pain shrugged and wore his face?
("We loved our darkies"—Cousin Dwight.)
I've since gone back up there. I knew the place.

Father and Mother, side by side tonight
Lax as dolls in your lit showcase,
Where are those poor souls now? Did they see right
Into our hearts at last, and know their place?

DOMINO

Delicious, white, refined
Is all that I was raised to be,
Whom feeling for the word
Plus crystal rudiments of mind
Still keep—however stirred—
From wholly melting in the tea.

Far, far away, men cut
The sea-wide, sea-green fields of cane.
Often a child's lament
Filled the infested hut.
Doña Pilar flew back for Lent
—Had she been inhumane?

The better to appraise his mess,
History's health freak begs
That such as we be given up.
Outpouring bitterness
Rewards the drainer of the cup . . .
He'll miss those sparkling dregs.

PALM BEACH WITH PORTUGUESE MAN-OF-WAR

for Tony Parigory

A mile-long vertebrate picked clean
To lofty-plumed seableached incurving ribs

Poor white the soil like talcum mixed with grit
But up came polymorphous green

No sooner fertilized than clipped
Where glimmerings from buried nozzles rose

And honey gravel driveways led
To the perpetual readiness of tombs

Shellwhite outside or white-on-white
A dropping bird motif still wet

Pastel and madrepore the shuttered rooms'
Nacreous jetsam wave on wave

Having swept our late excrescences
The wens and wives away to mirrorsmoke

Place settings for the skin
Diver after dark the extra man

Drowning by candlelight whose two minds reel
How to be potent *and* unsexed

Worth a million *and* expendable
How to be everybody's dish

And not have seen through the glass visor
What would be made of him some night

By the anemone's flame chiffon gown
Like those downtown in the boutiques

By razor labia of hangers-on
To territories this or that

Tiny hideous tycoon stakes out
Empire wholly built upon albino

Slaves the fossil globules of a self-
Creating self-absorbing scheme

Giddy in scope pedantic in detail*
Over which random baby gorgons

Float without perception it would seem
Whom their own purple airs inflate

And ganglia agonizingly outlive
Look out! one has been blown ashore

For tomorrow's old wet nurse to come
Ease from the dry breast and sheet in foam

---

*"Exactly like Egypt in the thirties," you marvel. ("The Nile without Cleopatra," Henry James had said.) But across the lake West Palm Beach tells a different story. Here are garages, trailer camps, fruit stands, TV bars. Here people actually live year round, or die—my father's buried in that old cemetery off the Interstate. Such rudiments as these make up a flat prose text, which dented fender or gouged stucco or the slash in a black forearm help, like punctuation, to render fully, finally intelligible.

THE SCHOOL PLAY

"Harry of Hereford, Lancaster, and Derby,
Stands here for God, his country, and . . ." And what?
"Stands here for God, his Sovereign, and himself,"
Growled Captain Fry who had the play by heart.
I was the First Herald, "a small part"
—I was small too—"but an important one."
What was not important to the self
At nine or ten? Already I had crushes
On Mowbray, Bushy, and the Duke of York.
Handsome Donald Niemann (now himself,
According to the Bulletin, headmaster
Of his own school somewhere out West) awoke
Too many self-indulgent mouthings in
The dummy mirror before smashing it,
For me to set my scuffed school cap at him.
Another year I'd play that part myself,
Or Puck, or Goneril, or Prospero.
Later, in adolescence, it was thought
Clever to speak of having found oneself,
With a smile and rueful headshake for those who hadn't.
People still do. Only the other day
A woman my age told us that her son
"Hadn't found himself"—at thirty-one!
I heard in the mind's ear an amused hum
Of mothers and fathers from beyond the curtain,
And that flushed, far-reaching hour came back
Months of rehearsal in the gymnasium
Had led to: when the skinny nobodies
Who'd memorized the verse and learned to speak it
Emerged in beards and hose (or gowns and rouge)
Vivid with character, having put themselves
All unsuspecting into the masters' hands.

REVIVALS OF *TRISTAN*

The loving cup was poisoned.
How is it that I knew?
Its drinkers before long—
Flagstad and Melchior
Or Fremstad and whoever,
Couple after couple
Drawn by the horseshoe magnet—
Lay quenched on the stage floor.
Small hands ached from applauding
A residue of song,
High pearly C's not wholly
Dissolved in that strong brew.

An old print: La Fenice
(The house burnt and rebuilt)
From center stage appears
Almost a bird—stalls each a
Copperplated feather;
Aisle a proud neck; the boxes
Blazing with glass and gilt
An outspread tail in tiers.
No "gods", no mortals—only
Those bright blank quizzing tracers
Anticipation aims
At the rekindled pair

For whom aigrette and shako
Climb tonight's torchlit stair,
To fan whose flames the posters
Torn off like Tristan's bandage
In his delirium
Are pasted with fresh names.
Soon throughout Western Europe
Until the first World War
In every garret room
A highly motivated
Young would-be Isolde
Takes up the fatal score.

Revivals of Tristan

What did I want? A golder,
Emptier cup, a grail
Quite plain within. Whoever
Lifted it would quail;
The fires of that iris
Focus and draw him down.
He now becomes *its* pupil,
Thirsty for the moment
When the parched gold abyss
Upheld amid the din
Swallows the human image
And huge wings clap in bliss.

DAYS OF 1941 AND '44

for David Mixsell

The nightmare shower room. My tormentor leers
In mock lust—surely?—at my crotch.
The towel I reach for held just out of reach,
I gaze back petrified, past speech, past tears.

Or Saturday night war games. Shy of the whole
Student body, and my own, I've hid
In the furnace room. His warning stokes my head:
This time, Toots, it's your pants up the flagpole!

And why, four-letter man, descend
To pick on me, in those days less than nothing,
A shaky X on panic's bottom line?

Imagine meeting now, here at the end—
You sheep-eyed, stripped of your wolf's clothing—
And seeing which came true, your life or mine.

At Silver Springs, that Easter break,
I'd noted "heavenly colors and swell fish"
—Mismarriage of maternal gush
To regular-guy. By evening: "Bellyache."

I was *fifteen?* Dear god. Page after page,
Fury and rapture, smudge and curlicue,
One ugly duckling waddled through
The awkward age.

A month of sundaes, gym excuses, play
("I got the part!!") and "long walk with S. J."
Locate the diarist away at school

Right after the divorce. Would brat-
tishness that ripe for ridicule
Ever be resorbed like baby fat?

"A lord of Life, a prince of Prose"—
Alliterations courtesy of Wilde.
Another year, with such as these to wield,
I won the Fourth Form Essay Prize.

In vain old Mr Raymond's sky-blue stare
Paled with revulsion when I spoke to him
About my final paper. "Jim,"
He quavered, "don't, *don't* write on Baudelaire."

But viewed from deep in my initial
Aesthetic phase, brought like a lukewarm bath to
Fizzy life by those mauve salts,

Paradises (and if artificial
So much the better) promised more than Matthew
Arnold. Faith rose dripping from the false.

My dear—yes, let that stand: you were my first
True hate. You whispering, the sadist's glee.
You lounging, buried in my diary—
Each phrase a fuse. I wanted you to burst.

Your cubicle across from mine was bleak
As when school opened. Oh, *you* didn't need
Cushions, posters, cotton for nosebleed,
A mother caught by flash in Red Cross chic.

Or did you? Three more years and you would die,
For lack of them perhaps, in France, at war.
Word reached me one hot twilight. It was raining,

Clay spattering the barracks. I
Fell back onto my bunk, parched for decor,
With *Swann's Way*. Basic training . . .

I'd have my France at war's end. Over highballs
Back home, would show that certain of us *were* up
To the museums and cafés of Europe—
Those peeling labels!

Rich boy you called me. True, there'd be no turning
Back from the mixed blessings of a first-rate
Education exquisitely offset
By an inbred contempt for learning.

And true, when money traveled, talent stayed
Deep in the trunk, assuming it got packed.
Mine was a harmless figment? If you like.

Remember, though, how untrained eyes subtract
From the coin-glint of a summer glade
The adder coiled to strike.

The nothing you'd become took on a weight
No style I knew could lighten. The latrine
Mirrors that night observed what once had been
Your mortal enemy disintegrate

To multiabsent and bone-tired hoplite,
Tamed more than told apart by his dog-tags.
Up the flagpole with those rank fatigues
Bunched round his boots! Another night

Beneath unsimulated fire he'd crawl
With full pack, rifle, helmeted, weak-kneed,
And peeking upward see the tracers scrawl

Their letter of atonement, then the flare
Quote its entire red minefield from midair—
Between whose lines it has been life to read.

PAGE FROM THE KORAN

A small vellum environment
Overrun by black
Scorpions of Kufic script—their ranks
All trigger tail and gold vowel-sac—
At auction this mild winter morning went
For six hundred Swiss francs.

By noon, fire from the same blue heavens
Had half erased Beirut.
Allah be praised, it said on crude handbills,
For guns and Nazarenes to shoot.
"How gladly with proper words," said Wallace Stevens,
"The soldier dies." Or kills.

God's very word, then, stung the heart
To greed and rancor. Yet
Not where the last glow touches one spare man
Inked-in against his minaret
—Letters so handled they are life, and hurt,
Leaving the scribe immune?

TOPICS

1. CASUAL WEAR

Your average tourist: Fifty. 2.3
Times married. Dressed, this year, in Ferdi Plinthbower
Originals. Odds 1 to 9^{10}
Against her strolling past the Embassy

Today at noon. Your average terrorist:
Twenty-five. Celibate. No use for trends,
At least in clothing. Mark, though, where it ends.
People have come forth made of colored mist

Unsmiling on one hundred million screens
To tell of his prompt phone call to the station,
"Claiming responsibility"—devastation
Signed with a flourish, like the dead wife's jeans.

2. POPULAR DEMAND

These few deep strongholds. Each with generator,
Provisions, dossiers. It would seem the worst
Has happened, who knows how—essential data
Lost in the bright, chromosome-garbling burst.

You, Comrade, will indefinitely be resident
Of this one, with your disciplined women and staff;
You and yours of this one, Mr. President.
Grim huddles. Then a first, uncertain laugh

—Spirits reviving, as life's bound to do?
Not from dead land, waste water, sulphur sky.
Nowhere is anything both alive and blue
Except, inside your block heads, the mind's eye

Marveling up out of our common grave:
You never thought . . . Sincerely didn't think . . .
Who gave it clearance? It ransacks the cave
For you with cordial venom. Damn you, drink!

3. CAESARION

A glow of cells in the warm Sea,
Some vaguest green or violet soup
Took a few billion days to loop
The loops we called Eternity.

Before the splendor bit its tail
Blake rendered it in aquatint
And Eddington pursued a glint—
Recoil, explosion—scale on scale.

What stellar hopefuls, plumed like Mars,
Sank to provincial rant and strut,
Lines blown, within the occiput?
Considering the fate of stars,

I think that man died happiest
Who never saw his Mother clasp
Fusion, the tiny naked asp,
By force of habit to her breast.

II

IDEAS

CHARLES and XENIA are discussing them
At her place. Interrupted solitaire,
Fern, teapot, humdrum harmonies from where
Blinks a green cat's-eye, the old FM.

XENIA: Now no. But when I am child my parents
Are receiving them. Emigrés I think very old,
Distinguished. Spectacles with rims of gold.
Clothes stained by acid of expérience.

Forever I am mixing them, although
My father explain, this one is physicist,
Archéologue, poet, so, down the list.
Tongues they are speaking sometimes I not know,

But the music! After dinner they are
Performing 18th century trio or quatuor
As how do French say digestif before
Mother is bringing in the samovar.

When they have finish tea they kiss, pif paf,
My father's both cheeks and my mother's hand—
Me too, if I go not yet to dreamland
So late bezaubert on my little pouf.

Maybe I visit Necropole in Queens
By underground with flowers once a year
To show respect. But they are buried here,
Here in my heart. CHARLES: Oh you Europeans. . . !

Mine by comparison are so, well, crude,
Self-pitying, opportunistic, young. Their gall
Is equaled only by that paradoxical
Need for acceptance the poor dears exude.

Ideas

I'm sitting quietly? Up roars the motorbike
Cavalcade—horns, goggles, farts of flame.
They swagger in as if their very name
Implied a nature seminal, godlike.

One strips. One dials Biloxi. One assumes
The lotus position; and all, that I am who
Was put on earth to entertain them. As I do.
You simply wouldn't believe the state of my rooms,

And the racket, and the 6 × 18 psychedelic
Daubs. Weeks on end, I'll shut my doors to even
The few I fancy. Can you think what heaven
It is not to have to hear the syllables "Tillich,

Hesse, Marcuse," at least not from their lips?
Back they go to the glassy Automat
They thought was the Ritz, before we met.
Just picturing them there, though, their collapse,

Without me, into vacancy, the joint
Stubbed out in ketchup, I begin to feel,
Well, sorry. How long since their last real meal?
And am I all that fond of needlepoint?

Besides, the simplest can appear—once dressed
In things of mine, and keeping their mouths shut—
Presentable. Not in smart places, but
You know my soft spot for the second best.

Enfin, considering the lives they've led,
They're shaping up. Some of my polish must
Be rubbing off on them. Now if they'd just
Learn to stick to their side of the bed—

Midnight already? I've a date. Bye. *Goes.*
The music stops. XENIA *resumes her Patience.*
VOICE: This performance of the Enigma Variations
Has brought our evening concert to a close.

THE "METRO"

One level below street, an airless tank—
We'd go there, evenings, watch through glass the world
Eddy by, winking, casting up
Such gorgeous flotsam that hearts leapt, or sank.

Over the bar, in polychrome relief,
A jungle idyll: tiger, water hole,
Mate lolling on her branch, apéritif-
Green eyes aglare. We also lolled and drank,

Joking with scarface Kosta, destitute
Sotíri, Plato in his new striped suit . . .
Those tigers are no more now. The bar's gone,
And in its place, O memory! a bank.

THE HOUSE FLY

Come October, if I close my eyes,
A self till then subliminal takes flight
Buzzing round me, settling upon the knuckle,
The lip to be explored not as in June
But with a sense verging on micromania
Of wrong, of tiny, hazy, crying wrongs
Which quite undo her—look at that zigzag totter,
Proboscis blindly tapping like a cane.
Gone? If so, only to re-alight

Or else in a stray beam resume the grand toilette
(Eggs of next year's mischief long since laid):
Unwearying strigils taken to the frayed,
Still glinting wings; the dull-red lacquer head
Lifted from its socket, turned mechanically
This way and that, like a wristwatch being wound,
As if there would always be time . . .

Downstairs in this same house one summer night,
Founding the cult, her ancestress alit
On the bare chest of Strato Mouflouzélis
Who stirred in the lamp-glow but did not wake.
To say so brings it back on every autumn
Feebler wings, and further from that Sun,
That mist-white wafer she and I partake of
Alone this afternoon, making a rite
Distinct from both the blessing and the blight.

AN UPSET

Drowsing in bed alone, quite thoughtless of nights
When I didn't, an ominous crack, some loud low snaps
    Like river ice breaking up
From the next room (lit still—I hadn't retired)
    Swept me out there in time to watch my
        Grandfather's table,
      One of the pedestal's three
        Leonine hips
    Disjointed under mounting stress,
        Collapse.

      It could have been
    The old man felled anew
      Seen through a thaw
Of pain—struck broadside, banks whose failure
    Sent slowly crashing full
Ashtray, lamp, magnifying glass and—no!—
Liszt; *Les Dieux*; *The Japanese Tattoo*;
    Babel's *Collected Stories*; *Last*
Poems; *Thinking* and *Willing* (boxed together);
Animal Farm; *A Little Boy Lost*—to name just a few.

    Whew. A disaster zone
Facing therapy: sandpaper, clamps and glue,
Jetsam and overflow's diversion to shelves
    Unbuilt, if not to plain
      Oblivion . . .
    Another "flood" behind us,
      Now to relearn
    Uprightness, lightness, poise:
First things—the lamp supposes, prone
    Yet burning wildly on.

MONTH

Sun-up off easterly casings prints a first
Sheet of pink, soon-to-be-cancelled commemoratives:
Liner with tugs, the old king's midair medallion
Balancing a new moon's in the next frame.
Or it's an edifice of frames and valances,
Noons, twilights, seven to a floor, arranging
For views (*12:30—G at the Flèche d'Or*)
Of someone permanently opposite,
Whose wallpaper is change; thin rain, the tinsel
Flocking of today's. Antagonist
And tenant both, across this neutral grid
Green and red forces monitor
She'd meet your eye. But names, claims, fleet o'clocks
(*Pick up opera tickets before 6*)
Forming between you like a frost,
Or like the TV's electronic blizzard
Phasing to terror in a ski-mask
Whatever cozy personality,
White out all glow of her interior,
All recollection that on high
Reigns cloudless glory, moon just past the full,
And stars. Unfelt, they even so
Strike through cover to the date. Tomorrow's
Four edges flush with a great furnace door
Go dark. Already the last act? One fugitive
Beam from that first, half-mythic dawn
Degenerates to limelight Dalibor
Falls bleeding in. Check. Don't make his mistake
And wish on the wrong crescent, lest her pawn
Turn queen and—Thunder scores. You've just this moment
Left to unriddle her new name, and wake.

SANTO

for Peter Hooten and Alan Moss Reverón

Francisco on his shelf,
Wreathed in dusty wax
Roses, for weeks and weeks
Hadn't been himself—

Making no day come true
By answering a prayer,
Just dully standing there . . .
What did our Grandma do?

She painted his beard black
And rinsed the roses clean,
Then hid his rags in half
A new red satin cloak,

Renaming him Martín.
Next week the baby spoke,
Juan sent a photograph
On board his submarine,

Aunt Concha went to cook
Downtown at the hotel,
The sick white dog got well
—And that was all it took!

PETER

Right arm: a many-splendored
Korean dagger-and-heart
Wound in a scroll, or banner—
DEATH BEFORE DISHONOR.

(Between the H and O
One barely audible
Stammer of skin,
DISH ONOR—so.)

Then left: italic *Lillia,* herself
Far out in Venice West
With the car and the children, sinking
Painlessly in

Under a BB shot
Probed to this white star
Through deepening north woods where "Spring was best"
And "never human foot . . ."

But your chest, a boy's no longer,
Paler, leaner
From night shifts at the Mill:
Across it still, over your real heart—rainbow

Fixes of plumage all that while postponed—
The USA's storm-blue
Project of an eagle
Glides, with nothing in its claws but you.

2. BAD TRIP

Gray light. A cautious tread.
Your weight
On the bedside, shuddering—
Eighty million comets in your head!

Walking all night
Beach after beach, surfstrafe,
Starknout, clockwise flailings of the dark . . .
I want to think we're safe,

Each of us, in each day's golden scales.
From your unwinking stare
A juice of pain
Trickles between knuckles. There,

The tranquilizer's working. There, lie back,
Hush. Tears
Wetting the pillow touch
Its featherbrain

And soon enough a suite for solo pharynx
Clumsily bowed and scraped will find me bent,
A room away, on putting words
Into an angel's mouth. Thirty-eight years

No less the waif
Afraid of dark? Sunshine
Spread over hurt feet, snore to your heart's content
And mine.

Peter

3. FUTURE APPLES INC.

You've fallen on work.
Luck smiles her little smile, by legerdemain
Those knuckles turn to outcrop,
Those tricklings to a wind-creased pool,

And here's your form
Reflected in a farm!—
Gaunt, lightly, chronically stoned
Latterday Eden with its absentee

Landlord, its wary creatures. The mud-caked brush-hog
Loves no man yet, neither (to judge by scratches
On wrists and calves)
Do the blackberry patches.

Some trees then, old as wives,
But bearing. And uphill, a beard
Of second growth, fruitless perplexities,
Dead roots, bygone

Entanglements *away* from light
Beg to be cleared.
It's winter wheat, clover and timothy,
Seasons of sweetening

If young limbs are to climb
Where a brow's furrowed, and the first-born so deftly
Hefts his bushel that you blink astonished
From time to time.

40

4. THE FIRST-BORN

—Of *this* union.
Fact is, you've children everywhere,
Vermont, Korea, some
Grown-up enough to have kids of their own,

For misspelt pleas to come—
Illness, abortion, welfare and parole.
They all need help.
You're sorry and would like to help

But figure you help them more in the long run
By not helping now.
And so you grin and shrug
As at the mention of vasectomy—

Genetic litterbug!
This latest batch is "different"—still unscarred
By life, you mean?
In drifts the six-year-old

Wearing his mother's blouse (where's she?
oh, "off on a rampage"),
Red polish on the fingernails
Of one hand. Drawn to me,

He lolls between my knees, asks *why* and *why*,
But listens also, much as if the die
Hadn't been cast. Will he have you—will I—
When all else fails?

Peter

5. "FIDELIO" FROM THE MET

Upon a certain rock
—Glacial warden over "dreams come true"—
You kept on building castles, no,
Dungeons in air,

Unspeakable, unvisitable glooms
Whose guiltless prisoner,
Wasted beyond recognition, was alive
Just barely, just because you were.

(How often in the city
I'd see you—boots, jeans, glasses, hair—
And shout. As if you could do better than
To look like everyman.)

Yet when that boulder you'd go sit on,
Peter, come night,
To smoke and watch the constellations
For its dislodging needed dynamite

And like the heaviest heart at freedom's trumpet
Leapt awkwardly an inch, and broke,
There was no question whose
Whole life, starwise along its faults, had started

To set the musical
Crystals, feldspar and quartz,
Aglow down pristine faces only now
Seeing the light.

A DAY ON THE CONNECTICUT RIVER

The billionth-or-so dawn,
And yet how primitive
The little factory looks, upstream,
Its brickwork that of "early man"

Launched and paddling through creation's
At-a-stroke venerable inventory
Baked into clay banks, bedded onto stone,
The day meanwhile our own.

Tire after scuttled tire
Glides under the canoe,
Manholes of a twilit avenue.
Better admire

The tannin-tinted clarity
—An opal freckle? A bug's wing—
Dimpled, asway, working
Cures for singularity,

Each view, to its least defect,
Flawlessly duplicated, healed . . .
Or was that last cornfield
Greener in reflection than in fact?

Duck! Museum
Skylight lowers
Like a boom. Through bowers
Of the no-see-um

One broad-bowed solo
Chord subtending, now,
Brindled cow,
Barn and silo,

A Day on the Connecticut River

Carries the Ur-
Conceptualist further
Into mimesis:
Life ever truer

To life, begun
Afresh with a few like-minded species,
While the rest of *ours* whizzes
Down Route 91

Whose traffic drone
(Or falls ahead?
Stay, reconnoiter
This white water—)

Yields to the eternal
Drumming of bees
In a noon tree's
Bleached bone.

Ah but, our zenith passed, my friend,
Two galley slaves, retracing a dead end
Of scum-glaze, lilypad, Atari dragonfly,
We're cuffed alert by headwind—empty sky—

Miles from a landing—every pulse a mean
Swipe of the palette knife—painstaking sheen
In jeopardy—the master's touch lost—sun
Cross-questioned, mutely reddening—damage done:

What good's "eternity" if it won't get
Us anywhere in time to build a fire
And pitch the tent and heat our stew before
Night falls, and share a final cigarette

Whereby new-smelted leads of the moonrise
Nonplus the prowling far-off headlight eyes,
And twin dreams fumble, ember and earth chill,
Shadow and cave, for one another—? Still

Once more in the event
All came to pass.
First light. Then, piece by piece,
Exact scales weigh the fortune lent

On such fair terms. From clay,
Cuneiform cliff swallows whistling dart—
Transaction noted here, in part—
Up and away.

LAST MORNINGS IN CALIFORNIA

Another misty one. These opaline
Emulsions of world and self. Paulette high up
In eucalyptus uttering her sun cry.
Arms reaching for the glimmer coming, going.

Tan shingle house, its hearth out cold, its tenant
Likewise, under patchwork. Fortune told
In Cups, a child on whom the Sun sweats fire,
The cards inverted, strewn, and his wild words

"Fool that one was and Hermit one now is,
Simple Death we'll both feel like tomorrow—"
Screwdrivers flecking the carpet with damp rust.
Of late a Guest, a further figure

Almost himself thanks to some B Complex
Taken in time, sits in the ferny alcove
Leafing a book of words Paulette appears to have learned
Never, never again to climb trees with.

She turns magnificent sane eyes upon this other's
Apparition. Strokes its grizzled beard
With gray-gloved fingers. Nearly gets to share
Its Danish when—a rent in air, the day's first

Thudding shudder (little hornet jet
Lonesome for Asia) sends the lemur flying
Into her master's limbs. His features dim and brighten
Working their way through night school. Every morning

The rip widens. At its edge a sun
Great white cloths equip will be wiping grime
From the tinted blue plate glass of fifty stories.
Perilous task. You wouldn't dare look down

On meditation center or shopping plaza.
One hard glance at the fault so many out here built on
And who knows? by noon another scarp upcoast,
Gilt broom and giant antennae, could be toppling

Dream material into some profounder
Pacific state—sea-boom, its thunder stolen
By the sleepers' softly breathing cave. Carnation
Pink to bone-white snippet stitched,

Laved past bleeding. Just one head, one tail
Protruding. Loud gin stilled and dyer's blues broadcast
On the spent wavelengths of the quilting bee . . .
Instead, the reader looks up "eucalyptus"

(From the Greek, *well-hidden*). Or if the sun has slipped
This once from its mile-high, breakneck ledge
To land somehow unhurt, all smiles,
Square in the suitcase he is living out of,

Goes—the cards have had him coming and going—
And kneels before the radiant disarray,
Clothing for days to come. On any one of them
Shutting the lid in a twinkling he'll be gone.

BRONZE

In August 1972 a skin-diver off Riace, on the Calabrian coast, saw at a depth of seven or eight meters an arm upthrust from the sandy bottom. Having made sure that it was not of flesh, and remarking nearby a second, sanded-over form, he notified the local Archeological Museum. Frogmen easily raised the two figures. Even encrusted with silica and lime, they were from the start felt to be Greek originals. Their restoration, in Florence, would take nine years.

I

Birdsong. May. Tuscany. A house. Sunset
Through red or green panes falling on small print
Pored over by two figures: my companion
("David the Fair") still, after all these years,
Marvelously young, gentle in manner—yet
A certain eager bloom is lost, like wax,
To earn a new, inexorable glint;
Umberto then, our host, gnarled round his cane,
Long freckled hands refolding the timetable
Dense as himself with station and connection.
Triumphant stumps of silver light
His austere satyr's face. The morning train
To Florence will allow us, he opines,
Forty minutes with them, "all one needs.
The next train down will have you back for lunch."

Perfection—they won't be in such easy reach
Ever again. But guess who hesitates!
"Close connections," says too quiet a voice,
"Harm the soul." I stare (indeed,
So he has always thought) and check a groan.
He's been unwell—one must remember that;
Has no resistance to cold, heat, fatigue,
Or anything, apparently, but me.
Fine! Say we never see them. I'm already
Half resigned. Half fuming also. These

Two halves, a look exchanged, now choose their weapons—
Notebook and cigarette—then step outside
To settle their affair beneath the trees.

The trees! Tall domed communicating chambers,
A dark flight above ground. One duellist
Writes blind: *my piano nobile.* The other
Levels his lighter, fires into the air,
Panicking the nearest green room where
Starlings by now have joined—safety in numbers—
Forces against the Owl. A twittering dither
Fills no less the wisdom-threatened mind . . .
The starlings, though, seem rather to rewind
Our day of human speech, erasing it
At treble speed from the highstrung cassette.
If one could do as much— A last drag. Wrong
To be so—so— Saved by the dinner gong.
I run to dip my hands in water first.
How pale they turn, how innocent, immersed.

2
Umberto's meal: a tablespoon of wine
Stirred into his minestra. While we cope
With eggs and spinach, fruit and cheese, he talks.
The life inside him's like a local clay
Gritty with names, Montale, Berenson,
Edith Wharton making our eyes flash
—Mario's too, who waits in his white jacket.
Plates gleam dimly from the walls' high gloom.
Our host's gaze lidded, voice a purr,
Out comes the story long heard *of.* I wash
It down tonight a shade too greedily—
Hence this impression in blurred chalk:
The famous story of Umberto's walk.

When Italy surrendered to the Allies
In 1943, September 3rd,

Bronze

The proclamation was five days deferred
Until their main force landed at Salerno.
It was imperative that liaison
Be made with them, in those five days, by (word
Meaning to me anything but certain) "certain
Anti-fascist groups." And as there were no
Lines of communication safe from the Germans,
"Withdrawn," but smelling Naples' every rat,
Umberto offered to get through alone.
The train he boarded, one warm dusk in Rome,
Left after midnight, crept an hour down
The unlit coast; sniffed peril, backed away;
Returned its passengers to Rome at dawn.

Next . . . a bus? a jeep? a peasant's cart?
The vehicle evaporates. Our friend
(To be imagined half a lifetime spryer,
Credentials drily folded to his heart,
Correct as now in city clothes—
Whatever garment, that surreal year,
Betrayed its wearer like an epithet,
Skewfoot, fleet of spirit, dressed in whose very
Visibility to glide unseen
Across a poppied or a blackened field,
A bullet- or a fullmoon-pitted square)
Kept haltingly advancing. Hillsides rang
With the cicada of one sunny parasang.

The social fabric and his place in it
Were such that he knew people everywhere—
People the war had sent like snails
Into their shells, to feed on books and air.
So the stale biscuit and tea-tainted water
Served by a scholar's maiden aunt or sister
Brought him, through a last long stretch of dark,
Face to face with—tree-tall in lamplight—
"A type of Roman hero, your Mark Clark,

Beside whom on the Prefettura balcony,
His forces having landed overnight,
I megaphoned next morning—as my one
And only 'moment' on a balcony—
The terms of peace, translated, to the crowd."

"You were the hero," David murmurs, wowed.

3
Now Florence? But a stratagem
We only later analyze—
Bared shoulder and come-hither shrug
Of hill, the spread of golden thighs—
Lures our rented Fiat bug
Away from Them.

And soon enough, to two ecstatic
Oh's, on the horizon shines
Then vanishes, then shines again,
One of those metaphysical lines
Blue-penciled through the pilgrim's brain—
The Adriatic.

Our spirit-level, salt of life!
(Unpack the picnic here?) Above
Lie field and vineyard, castle built
To nurture intellect, art, love
Together with, let's face it, guilt,
Deception, strife.

Below, in brilliant aquarelle,
Undulating dullness fans
Itself to tatters. Bubble-streamers
Betray the scuba-superman's
Downward bent or Jungian dreamer's
Diving bell.

Bronze

Here at my desk, but fathoms deep,
I've known the veer and shock of schools,
The kiss of inky Mafiosi;
Perusing stanzas like tide pools,
Have seen the stranger flex a rosy
Mussel heap,

And shaken myself clear. The break
Of glib, quicksilver levity,
The plunge of leaden look or phrase
Thudding to rest where none can see . . .
I name just two of the world's ways
Picked by mistake.

Sheathed in a petrifying mitt,
A hand took mine on the sea floor.
That detour (we'll reach Florence yet)
Had to be structural before
Heroes tomorrow stripped of threat
Could rise from it.

4
—Not a moment, poor babies, too soon!
For the Mediterranean will in
Another few decades have perished,
And with it those human equivalents,
Memory, instinct, whatever
In you the first water so joyously
Answered to. These you have fed
To your desktop computers—e basta.
Yes, hard on the heels of God's death,
As reported in Nietzschean decibels,
Follows (writes Mary McCarthy
In Birds of America) *one*
Far more ominous bulletin: Nature
Is dead, or soon will be. And we
Are well out of it, who in the tempest—

Exultantly baring through coppery
Lips the carnivorous silver—
Knew best how to throw around weight
And go overboard. Thus we arrived
At the couch of the green-bearded ancient
To suffer the centuries' limpet
Accretions unwelcome as love
From a weakling, cold lessons imparted
Through waves of revulsion, yet taken
How deeply to heart! From their oozy
Sublime we have risen. Dissolving
The clay at our core, sonar probe and
Restorative poultice have brought
The high finish in which we began
Back to light. Your nostalgia completes the
Illusion with flickering tripods,
Where feasters, fastidious stucco
Pilasters, and vistas of shimmering
Water red roses rope off
Make us objects of art. We dislike it
As women in your day dislike
Being sexual objects, but were not
Consulted. To fictive environments
Blood is the fee. And this light,
This pink gel we peer out through (not gods
Like the hurler of levin in Athens,
Not tea-gowned ephebes like the driver
At Delphi, but men in their prime
With the endocrine clout so rebarbative
To the eternally boyish
Of whichever sex) is the shadow of
Light we once lived by, dealt death in,
Dividing the spoils. And it burns
But to spangle the gulf that expires
Between you—still crusted with appetite,
Armed to the teeth by your pitiful
Wish not to harm—and ourselves

Bronze

Whose much-touted terribilità
Is at last this articulate shell
Of a vacuum roughly man-sized. We
Should rather be silent. Rhetorical
Postures, the hot line direct
To the Kremlin or out of Hart Crane,
Leave us cold. It's for you to defuse them.
For us, in our Dämmerung swarming
With gawkers, what trials of mettle
Remain?—short of meltdown your fantasies
Trigger, then grandly shrug off
With a sangfroid our poor old heroics
Were child's play beside. Go. Expect no
Epiphany such as the torso
In Paris provided for Rilke. Quit
Dreaming of change. It is happening
Whether you like it or not,
So get on with your lives. We have done.

5
Let's do. From the entropy of Florence, dead
Ends, wrong turns, *I told you so*'s, through rings
First torpid then vertiginous, our route
Leads outward into the bright spin of things.
Our separate routes. A month. A year.
Time for Umberto, hobbling under plane
Trees now, now cypressed-in by memory,
To take a last step, crumple, disappear.
Time for Fair David to regain
A small adobe fortress where, beset
By rodent insurrections, howl and hoot,
He turns his skylit oils to the wall rain
Exorbitantly gutters. Time for me,

Who off and on had idolized these two,
To heed a sympathetic twinge.
The doctor probes and listens. Powers failing?

A shot of hormone? The syringe he fills,
At tip one shining droplet, pure foreplay,
Sinks into muscle. And on the third day
Desire floods the old red studio.
A figure reincarnate, wings outspread,
Full quiver, eager lips, from years ago—
My Eros to the life—awaits unveiling.
Friends, here is salvation! Are you blind?
Here, *under* the dumb layers which unwind
I somehow cannot. Tanglingly opaque,
They're nothing if not me. The hidden god,
Unknelt-to, feels himself to be a fake,

The poorest jerky newsreel of dead forces
Breast-deep in waves, that strained for shore,
Bayonets flashing, helmeted young faces
Mad to provoke from the interior
Those attitudes assumed in love and war—
All fair, till peace limps forward on a cane.
The Axis fell. Its partners rose again.
Up came from vaults, for light to kiss awake,
The groggy treasures of the Glyptothek.
Out came war babies. Only the lost life
Held back, reduced to skeletal belief,
Coils of shot film, run-down DNA.
Earth saw to it as usual, clay to clay.

6
All fair? Precisely what, fair friend, umpteen
Stanzas your distance tinges haven't been.
You whom night strips to armature, whom day
Equips with tones to brush desire away,
Painting as much of sheer Experience
(Your holy mountain, that sea-born, immense
Magnet, its fatalities untold)
As one tall window facing north can hold,

Raptly, repeatedly have scaled it, if
Only to canvas. Metamorphs of cliff,
Quarry and timberline, you understand,
Haunt me, too. Come then, "because they're there,"
On with our stories. Make the telling fair.
But first, in all but liaison—this hand.

7
Off the record, but as everyone
Perfectly knew, Umberto was the son
Of his father's friend the King, whose name he bore.
A discreet match, the death of the young bride,
This phantom parentage on either side . . .
Rumor? Yet the King's bust, I recall,
Kept reigning, on its trophied pedestal,
Head and shoulders over a salon
Never in use (gilt horrors, plush, veneer),
The single, token room to have been done
Up for the Contessa. Her demise
Preserved in prelapsarian Empire
And Biedermeier the enchanting rest:
Stained glass and goat-foot chair, blue willows peeling
From gesso'd wall, tent-stripes or clouds from ceiling.

Blows that set our braver products clanging
Level categorically these hanging-
By-a-thread gardens of the West.
Umberto first intended the estate
As a "retreat for scholars." His last will
Left it intact to Mario the butler,
So long devoted and his brood so great.
The house sighed. It had entertained the subtler
Forms of discourse and behavior. Still,
There'd be the baby's tantrum, the wife's laugh,
The old man's groan. New blood. How else redeem
Spells of such cast and temper as to seem
Largely the stuff of their own cenotaph?

8
For in the odd hour made even
Odder as it dawns,
I too exist in bronze.
We were up on the deck, drinking
With summer friends, when Fred
Asked who the bust was of.
Year-round sentinel
On the domestic ramparts,
Acquiring pointlessness
As things we live with do,
It gave me a look back:
The famous, cold, unblinking
Me at six, I said—
Then drifted from his side
To stand by it. Ah yes.

Slowly the patina
Coarsened, paled—no perch
For owl or nightingale.
The local braggart gull
Flaps off and up, its shriek
Leaving a forelock white.
Where the time's flown I wonder.
A deeply-bored eye sees,
Or doesn't, the high trees
Waving in vain for sundry
Old games like Hide and Seek
Or Statues to be played,
Come evening, in their shade.

Losses of the foundry!
As chilling aftermath
Laszlo—my sculptor—made
Headlines one morning: QUEENS
MAN AXED BY SONS. Had they
Also posed for him,
Two trustful little boys. . . ?

Bronze

Smoothing their brows, the maker's
Hypnotic fingertips
(I still feel my scalp crawl)
Were helpless to forestall
The molten, grown-up scenes
Ahead, when ire and yearning,
Most potent of alloys
Within us, came to grips.

Here Augie, seeing me absent,
Ambled up to rest
Tanned forearms easily
On my unruffled hair.
A tilted beer, a streak
Staining bluegreen my cheek—
Bless him, he couldn't care
Less for the Work of Art!
The stubborn child-face pressed,
Lips parted, to the heart
Under his torn T-shirt
Telling the world *Clean Air
Or Else*, was help and hurt
As much as I could bear.

III

CHANNEL 13

It came down to this: that merely naming the creatures
        Spelt their doom.
Three quick moves translated camelopard, dik-dik, and
        Ostrich from
Grassland to circus to Roman floor mosaic to
        TV room.

Here self-excusing voices attended (and music,
        Also canned)
The lark's aerobatics, the great white shark's blue shadow
        Making sand
Crawl fleshwise. Our ultimate "breakthrough" lenses took it
        In unmanned.

Now the vast shine of appearances shrinks to a tiny
        Sun, the screen
Goes black. Anaconda, tree toad, alpaca, clown-face
        Capuchin—
Launched at hour's end in the snug electronic ark of
        What has been.

THE BLUE GROTTO

for Mona Van Duyn

The boatman rowed into
That often-sung impasse.
Each visitor foreknew
A floor of lilting glass,
A vault of rock, lit blue.

But here we faced the fact.
As misty expectations
Dispersed, and wavelets thwacked
In something like impatience,
The point was to react.

Alas for characteristics!
Diane fingered the water.
Don tested the acoustics
With a paragraph from Pater.
Jon shut his eyes—these mystics—

Thinking his mantra. Jack
Came out with a one-liner,
While claustrophobiac
Janet fought off a minor
Anxiety attack.

Then from our gnarled (his name?)
Boatman (Gennaro!) burst
Some local, vocal gem
Ten times a day rehearsed.
It put us all to shame:

The astute sob, the kiss
Blown in sheer routine
Unselfconsciousness
Before one left the scene . . .
Years passed, and I wrote this.

FROM THE CUTTING-ROOM FLOOR

Thanks, Dr Williams, my throat feels better already.
ANY TIME. I WASN'T IN THE AUDIENCE
WHEN YOU READ YR OPUS Oh dear— PLEASE DE NADA!
NEITHER WAS WHITMAN. WE SULKED IN OUR TENTS:
'BILL, I MADE DO WITH A DOORWAY IF IT HAD A
LILAC OR A HANDSOME LAD IN IT,
YOU WITH A SMALL TOWN & BABIES. GUESS WE MISSED
THE TRAIN?' But you were . . . America! LAND OF THE FREE
SAMPLE, HOME OF THE (GRADE B) RAVE. FADS, FADS:
WHAT HAPPENED TO THE BEATNIKS? KEROUAC
WAS HERE, MADE A BRIEF TRUCKER'S STOP Then? BACK.
WHAT WOULD HAVE KEPT HIM? I ENVIED BODENHEIM
HIS HOUR OF FAME. WHERE'S OLD MAX NOW? A BLACK
CANE WORKER IN CUBA. *Your* star, though, would seem
Fixed in our skies. YOU KNOW WHY? WHITMAN. 'BY GOD
(HE SAID) BILL STAYS OR I GO BACK WITH HIM!'
Good for you both! I MISS LIFE. LIFE WAS GOOD.
Well, can't we always botch our lives in order
Just to be born again, time after time?
NOT IF THE STAR CHUGS OFF & LEAVES ITS BOARDER.

★

I felt your presence yesterday, Miss Moore,
But lost you in the crush. TOM ELIOT
GAVE ME YOUR KIND THOUGHTS. We had hoped to hear
Your own. May we? O? WELL! THERE'S SUCH A NEED
FOR CHLOROPHYLL, SOME OF US WORK AT HUMUS DEPOTS
TRYING TO EVEN OUT THE 'GOOD' AND 'BAD'.
BACTERIAL MOULDS ARE SAVAGE, LIVE, MINUTE
WORLDS GOING FIERCELY AT EACH OTHER. WE
TRY FOR, O YOU KNOW, PEACE CONFERENCES?
TOM LAUGHS. WELL, LANGUAGE, LOVELY HOW IT RUNS
AWAY WITH YOU. AH NOW HE DOESN'T LAUGH.
HERE IT'S A VELVET BLACKNESS GIVEN TO THOUGHT,

BUT WE'VE OUR LITTLE GET-TOGETHERS. YOU
FINISH A WORK, OR PLATO LEAVES, OR YOUNG
MR LOWELL ARRIVES: A PARTY. OTHERS FAR
LESS FORMAL: SAY I'M BENT OVER A SLIDE
SUGGESTING . . . TROUBLE? THINGS AT ODDS? & THINK
SOMETHING THERE IS THAT TRULY NEEDS A WALL,
& THERE'S RF: 'YOU CALLED ME, MARIANNE?'
'YES, ROBERT, YOUR POEM'S WRONG.' DON'T WE GO AT IT!
You always need the live occasion, then—
A death, a poem, a bacterial strain.
HERE, YES, WE BOUNCE OFF LIFE. IT'S OUR TELSTAR.
BUT ALSO, WE WHOSE LIVES WERE SPENT 'CREATING'
(O WEARY WORD) SEEM BUT A TOUCH AWAY.
From? LIFE. EACH OTHER. OFTEN I THINK, WHY NOT
JUST ASK M. LAFONTAINE TO HELP WITH THAT?
'CHERE MADEMOISELLE, ME VOICI' AND WE CHAT.
In French? MINE'S BAD. HIS ENGLISH WORSE. WE TALK
IN PERFECT THOUGHT, FAR EASIER THAN TALK.

THIS HOUR IS A REFRESHMENT. WHEN I SAT
WITH DJUNA THE RESULTS WERE TERRIFYING!
DJUNA OF COURSE LIKED A LOW CROWD. SHE REVELLED
IN STRANGLED MESSAGES: 'THEY HADN'T OUGHT
TO'VE HUNG ME' ETC. 'DJUNA, ENOUGH!'
RAT SQUEAKS, I TOLD HER. You were right, I fear.
I FEAR SO TOO. WITH ONLY NOW & THEN
THE GENTEEL MOUSE. Funny . . . pure Lafontaine.
ISN'T IT ODD? I WONDER NOW AT ALL
THAT MAKING-HUMAN OF THE ANIMAL.
And its reverse, as feral natures roam
Our ever dimmer human avenue.
GERTRUDE CRIED OUT TO ME AS WE LEFT YOUR DO:
'CAREFUL, MY DEAR, DON'T GET MUGGED GOING HOME!'

★

Elvis Presley "meets the press"
In Heaven. Hostess, Gertrude Stein—
Expatriate Mother of Them All.
YOU FROM THE PAPERS HUH he wonders. She:
(POOR BLOATED BOOBY   WHAT A MESS,
AT LEAST MY EMBONPOINT WAS MINE)
PITY YOUR TIME'S SHORT   NICE OF YOU TO CALL!
B4 YOU GO, A CUP OF NULLITY?

He hates this: WHERE R THE CAMERAS   ITS LIKE
NOTHING HERE   NO DRESSINGROOM   LIKE WHERE
AM I   WHERE R THE FANS   Thin air
Manages to coax from the dead mike
Aksel Schiøtz singing a Schubert song.
LISTEN   NO WAY   LIKE WHAT THE FUCK IS WRONG

★

AS WITH THE HOUSE CAT THE HOUSE PLANT DRINKS U IN. THAT
        RUBBER
TREE NEAR YR GOLD FRAME IS NOW QUITE DENSE WITH LONG
        REMEMBRANCE
—Of our neglect. How small its leaves have grown!
Why didn't we repot it years ago?
YET THIS CONTRACTED OLD NUMBER LONG IN THE TOOTH WILL GO
ON SHRINKING/THINKING. HAS IT SHRUNK BACK OUT OF OUR WAY?
Back from the mirror's door ajar, aglow,
Into your realm—an old, old image, no?
                                        OLD
AS THE LEGEND OF NARCISSUS FALLEN INTO THE DEATH
OF HIS OWN IMAGE. FOR THE IMAGE IN YR MIRROR IS
NOT YOU BUT REVERSED, TIMELESS: ONLY ONE MOMENT IN 10,
000 DO YOU NOTE THE CHANGE IN TIME. THE MIRROR WORKS TO
DECEIVE. IT MUST. FOR THE VANISHT FAERY FOLK ARE NO MORE
ELUSIVE THAN THE VANISHING YOU. AS MERCURY WE
HOLD FAST & HYPNOTIZE THOSE CERTAIN VALUABLE ONES
PEERING AT US WITH INCREASED DESPAIR SAYING 'CURIOUS,

THE EYE'S CLEAR WOODLAND POOL CLOUDED WHERE A FAUN DRANK
    & FLED,
THAT TEMPLE GONE FROM ONYX TO MARBLE, YES, PASSING
    STRANGE.'

    GREAT MAGIC, EH ENFANTS? FASCINATION'S UNBLINKING
    RABBIT PULLED FROM THE OPERA HAT OF CHANGE

★

. . . BUT DRAT, I'VE QUITE FORGOTTEN Robert, shame!
No mind left, there in the realm of Total Recall?
MIND ON THE THRESHOLD OF A NEW LIFE KEEPS
THE DEATHWATCH OVER ITS REMAINS OR NOT
AS IT SEES FIT. MINE'S RATHER LIKE THE FAMOUS
RUSTY-BOTTOMED COLANDER. The famous what?
ISN'T IT FAMOUS? (Voices: MR ROBERT,
WHAT FAMOUS RUSTY-BOTTOMED COLANDER?)
NOW NOW, JUST BECAUSE I'M GIRT BY DIMMER WITS . . .
I GIVE YOU WALLACE STEVENS, AN AUTHORITY
ON THE WHOLE SUBJECT *If* he remembers. JM
A CIVIL TONGUE BEHIND THOSE TEETH!
                         AHEM:
THIS OBJECT WAS DISCOVERED WHEN A CLUMP
OF ROYALTIES RISING FROM LUNCH AT SANDRINGHAM
PRAISING THE CURRY, ITS UNIQUE FLAVOR, ITS RICH
COLOR, FOLLOWED THEIR HOSTESS INTO THE KITCHEN
TO THANK (A SIGNAL HONOR) THE INDIAN COOK.
'I'VE BROUGHT IT FROM MY VILLAGE, MAM' THE SPICE?
'NO MAM, THE INSTRUMENT' & TO SICKLY PLUMP
RESPONSES OUT CAME THE FAMOUS R B C!
So our corroding minds give *these* concoctions
Their je ne sais quoi? AND MANY A MAJESTY
UP HERE AT LEAST, MANY A NASTY SHOCK

(And so forth. An antacid tone like Tums.
We hang on those lips, two flaky mediums.)

★

One evening in April '79
At table, mulling over cuts and changes
I have in mind—though DJ disagrees—
To make before the *Pageant* goes to press,
We ask our Lord of Light to arbitrate.

FROM HALF ACROSS THE WORLD, SCRIBE, HAND,
LIGHTING GAUNT LIVES IN JAIPUR, KINDLING THAT PEAK
OF POLISH ON A HOUSEWIFE'S BRASS TEAKETTLE,
OPENING A BABY'S (NO, NOT THAT ONE'S) EYES,
I SAY: HAND, YOU ARE WRONG. WE LIGHTERS-UP
KNOW THE MIND'S COBWEBS. IN THAT BALLROOM SCENE
O GLORY WHERE I PLAYED OUR MISTRESS' FOOL,
THE POINT WAS, LET THE (BLURRED) BRIGHT POINT REMAIN.
OUR AUDIENCE, REMEMBER, WERE THE DEAD.
WHO AMONG THEM, OF A SUNNY DAY,
COULD TOTTER TO THE POSTBOX: 'CHER CONFRERE,
ABOUT YR SECTION 6 I MEANT TO ADD . . .'
NO, IN THE BALLROOM A LATE CONGREGATION
SAT CONGRATULATING ITSELF UPON
(FACE IT, DEAR HAND) AN ARDUOUS TASK DONE.
THE BALLROOM, AH! COULD I BUT KISS ONCE MORE
THOSE DIMWIT FACES WITH THE DAWN!
BUT THEY HAVE HAD THEIR DAY (& SAY). THEREFORE
CHANGE AND CHANGE, O SCRIBE! COME UP TO THIS
INSTANT (FOR YOU INKY) AT MY HEIGHT
AS TOUCHING THE HIMALAYAS I DEFINE,
MORE, REFINE THEM, FOLD ON FOLD, FOREVER
GETTING AT THEIR BONE OF MEANING. CHANGE!
REVISE, RISE, SHINE! GOOD AH MY CHILDREN NIGHT!

ARCLIGHT

By day unlit, the magic helmet keeping
Its lord invisible, now at dusk leaps forth,
Air darkens round, less after all (despite
Ambit and atomies magnesium-bright)
A person than a presence of sheer mind
Which, in itself however genial,
Brought once more to bear upon the scene—
Glassglint, palmetto, crabgrass between cracks,
And, glowering feebly at its pale, five shacks—
Arrays our dim old crossroads in a dread
Exceeding dark's own. This discourager
Alike of stealth and star has come to do
By night. The dog it dusts asleep or dead.
Wings battering the naught it makes to shine.

RADIOMETER

At sunrise on a pin
Upright within a globe
No bigger than your frontal lobe
Four little blades of tin begin to spin.

One side of each is white
And one side black—
White knowing only to fend off,
Black only to drink in, drink in the light

At first with circumspection, then be hurled
Backwards by noon at dizzying speed
Through the revolving door that gives onto the world;

While forward, just as helplessly,
Ghost-faces hurtle—Yang and Yin?
Phlegm and fervor? You/me?

World without end?
Not this one. Look: the setting sun, my friend.

TREES LISTENING TO BACH

Overture. A shutter opens. Down
Goes light. The Norfolk Island pine
Potted in peatmoss breathes
Deeply once; resigns itself on cue.
Under the dimming dervish crown
Extend now four, no, five fringed limbs
(Twelve more hang downward barely skirting trance)
In stills—in stills that—yes! inspired
Revolve and quicken. As though fingers flew,
Each organ point's plump quiver
Already stitching, radiance
Turning to raiment and back, forth steps a spine
Threadbare in seams picked out by the moonrise.

Wonders who'll itemize? Why, the jade tree,
Budding collector grown
Roundshouldered from its decade in the shade,
A shut-in life. Though short on fun,
It takes note, missing none.
Some nine score pitch-pure, stone-smooth lobes
Store the Courante, the Sarabande's grave strobes.
Exact dynamics are its law,
And juicy, time-consuming pedantry
Its lesson. Fluke or flaw,
Dust in a groove, temptation to emote
And blot performance leaving it unswayed,
Its roc's claw grips a base that creeps clockwise.

Not so two chestnuts in the streetlamp's glow
Champing, manes tossing. No
Obstacle brooked: RUSH to developer
These multiple exposures, bring the sheaf,
Or by now trunkful, up to date
As if their whole belief

70

Racing each night a green crosscountry inch
Depended on it. Time—do they suspect?—
Is changing signature and only stable
These random moments ridden, then reined in,
As now, foam-petal-flecked,
Splattering triplets . . . Here the Gigue dismounts.
The stillness reaches "to the skies".

On the used plate a wash of silver dries.

PAUL VALÉRY: PALME

Veiling, barely, his dread
Beauty and its blaze,
An angel sets warm bread
And cool milk at my place.
His eyelids make the sign
Of prayer; I lower mine,
Words interleaving vision:
—Calm, calm, be ever calm!
Feel the whole weight a palm
Bears upright in profusion.

However its boughs yield
Beneath abundance, it
Is formally fulfilled
In bondage to thick fruit.
Wonder and see it grow!
One fiber, vibrant, slow,
Cleaving the hour fanwise,
Becomes a golden rule
To tell apart earth's pull
From heaven's gravities.

Svelte arbiter between
The shadow and the sun, *oracular*
It takes much sibylline
Somnolent wisdom on.
Unstintingly to suffer
Hails and farewells, forever
Standing where it must stand . . .
How noble and how tender,
How worthy of surrender
To none but a god's hand!

The lightest gold-leaf murmur
Rings at a flick of air,
Invests with silken armor
The very desert. Here
This tree's undying voice
Upraised in the wind's hiss,
As fine sand sprays and stings,
To its own self is oracle
Complacent of the miracle
Whereby misfortune sings.

Held in an artless dream
Between blue sky and dune,
Secreting, dram by dram,
The honey of each noon,
What is this delectation
If not divine duration
That, without keeping time,
Can alter it, seduce
Into a steady juice
Love's volatile perfume?

At moments one despairs.
Should the adored duress
Ordain, despite your tears,
A spell of fruitlessness,
Do not call Wisdom cold
Who readies so much gold,
So much authority:
Rising in solemn pith
A green, eternal myth
Reaches maturity.

These days which, like yourself,
Seem empty and effaced
Have avid roots that delve
To work deep in the waste.

Paul Valéry: *Palme*

Their shaggy systems, fed
Where shade confers with shade,
Can never cease or tire,
At the world's heart are found
Still tracking that profound
Water the heights require.

Patience and still patience,
Patience beneath the blue!
Each atom of the silence
Knows what it ripens to.
The happy shock will come:
A dove alighting, some
Gentlest nudge, the breeze,
A woman's touch—before
You know it, the downpour
Has brought you to your knees!

Let populations be
Crumbled underfoot—
Palm, irresistibly—
Among celestial fruit!
Those hours were not in vain
So long as you retain
A lightness once they're lost;
Like one who, thinking, spends
His inmost dividends
To grow at any cost.

LENSES

I. CONTACTS

Light as parentheses, your scales
(If not quite true so far
For weighing things "exactly as they are",
OK for skills

And situations) float
Insensibly on unshed tears . . .
One spark of dust? Quick, the extinguishers!
A stare afire, an entire flight

—Out, out! Their little drum's
Twin lids unscrew to let them soak.
And (look) here comes the Sandman with his sack
Of love and dreams.

2. MICROSCOPIC

The club is tiny, hard to locate. No
Neon sign, no noise.
You need immense focus and poise
To catch its minstrel show:

Nonstop cakewalk of multiple-jointed
Carbon-featured end-
Man enzymes, each with mirror friend
And high on his personal acid. Disappointed?

Still out to bridge the chasm?
But the strict program will not cease to size
You up, enucleate your inmost eye's
Nostalgie du protoplasme.

Lenses

3. TELESCOPE

Mark tonight's variation *Maggiore. Lento.*
Clear. Cold. The heavens' hushed, centrifugal evasion
Of the bungled hospitality we call vision.
Even should one of their company, entering the lean-to

Cloaked in a darkness bygone splendors break through,
Begin—O my swineherd!—the retelling, his itinerary
Is simply too complicated, too remote and solitary
For any human mind to stay awake through.

Yes, it was more than you or I could have imagined
Without the sense that made an old black pointer
Dozing by your embers twitch upright, and know the Hunter
And earn this dusty corner of his legend.

4. CAMERA

Eyes wild, hair midnight-tangled, robe in disarray,
Convulsed by sobs, or laughter:
Once again they've photographed her,
That everlasting woman led away

From—flash! As background blurs,
Hands out of nowhere reach for tomorrow's saint.
Which terrible, which heaven-sent
Passion was hers—

Stark grief, stark frenzy, stark
Helpless amusement? All of these?
Not to be outfaced by journalese,
Print her next likeness in your own red dark.

IN THE DARK

Come, try this exercise:
Focus a beam
Emptied of thinking, outward through shut eyes
On X, your "god" of long ago.

Wherever he is now the photons race,
A phantom, unresisting stream,

For nothing lights up. No
Sudden amused face,
No mote, no far-out figment, to obstruct
The energy—
               It just spends
And spends itself, and who will ever know

Unless he felt you aim at him   and ducked

Or you before the session ends
Begin to glow

MIDSUMMER EVENING ON THE PRINSENGRACHT

for Hans

It's late. The sun
Gone down, the scene remains—
Lintel, cornice, roof
Annealed in proof;

Idle each block-and-tackle
There at the apex of so many panes;
Cloud and clock tower one
With counterpremises the moon

Sleepwalks, and arches (doubled now to black
Silver-rimmed lenses of the blind) festoon . . .
Friend at last young, indeed
Almost a son,

Here it's your poems I can't read
That light lamps, fling up sashes, row beneath
Quickened, this quarter hour,
By the old tower,

Chime on chime on chime
—Percussions unresolved, conciliatory,
As if, still thinking out their story,
To ask for time.

SANTORINI: STOPPING THE LEAK

Five sessions of God willing lethal x
Rays on a live target purple-inked
For isolation, and the plantar wart
(Girt by its young, one throbbing multiplex
Neither knife nor acid could abort)
Active half my adult life's extinct
—Whereupon, sporting a survivor's grin,
I've come by baby jet to Santorin.

Inches overhead, a blue that burns,
That all but blackens—heaven as a flue?—
Against this white that all but calcifies.
Behind, a breakneck mile of hairpin turns,
The Golden Climb—mule dung and reek, whips, flies—
Lurches and jolts. Each moment someone new
Arrives at this despaired-of-from-below
Village unmelted on the crest like snow.

A gentler view, south from my balcony:
Past cubes and domes the baked vine terraces
Descend to beaches' black volcanic sand
And pewter glare of the September sea.
Mechanically a pencil guides my hand,
Then bells ajangle through the diocese
Bring the next balcony to life. Who's there?
Nelláki toweling her short silver hair.

She's not been idle, not our girl. It seems
We come provided with an introduction
To three old maiden sisters here, who set
A table that exceeds her wildest dreams
Of gourmandise. The ladies must be met,
And to that end I fear she's taken action:
Dispatched a note. A day or two should bring
Their summons. Meanwhile, homework, sightseeing!

Santorini: Stopping the Leak

The reason I've not made this trip before
Is that it would be—is—magnificent.
One wanted the companion who might
Act on a hushed injunction, less to ignore
The worst than stroll through it by evening light,
Made into courtyards (whitewashed, some for rent)
Where even stone-deaf Nelly hears her name
Spoken by mute bursts of nasturtium-flame.

Which color added, I've prepared my palette—
White, silver, black, night purple, dab of lake
For cliff-coagulations that regress
To null mist at a blow from the moon mallet.
Brushes? These five of mine with nothingness
Threatening forever to unmake
The living form it sees through in a trice—
A challenge to hold steady, these suffice.

Innermost chaos understood at first
As Gaia's long-pent-up emotions crippling
Her sun-thrilled body, spun to the great Lyre;
Pent up, but all too soon unleashed—outburst
Savage enough to bury in its fire
The pendant charms she wore, palace and stripling,
A molten afterbirth transmuting these
Till Oedipus became Empedocles—

Leaper headlong into that primal scene
And deafening tirade. The mother tongue
At which his blood boiled, his brain kindled. Ash
Of afterthought where once the sage had been,
Louse in a log . . . Or else, supposing flesh
Withstood temptation, could a soul that clung
To its own fusing senses crawl at last
Away unshriveled by the holocaust?

The curtain on a universal hiss
Would fall; steam cover all; millennia pass.
An island surface. Two. Three. Vineyards wax.
The plume of smoke with airier emphasis
Slant from the inky crater. Paperbacks
About Atlantis map the looking-glass
Rim of that old disaster, deep salt blue
Unrippling oval noon sun peers into.

Apart from the volcano and the wine,
The place, I read, was famous for its vampires.
People we inquire of shrug and stare—
No matter. Clearly, as the gods decline,
An eerie radiation fills the air
And eats their armor.The Byzantine Empire's
Avian-angelic iridescence
Shrank to black flitterings in the lymph of peasants.

Nelly agrees, but wears a child's gold cross
One hadn't seen, and wants to start with snails
Smothered in garlic. She's put in her hearing
Aid—we can talk. Out of the blue the loss,
Young, of her twin brother flickers, searing
Us both an instant; then her gaze drops. Veils
Of sheer belated comprehension blur
This little tumbler lifted, drunk to her.

Dear soul. Maria called her La Petite.
She has a modesty of scale and scope,
No use for buried motives, double vision:
Not one, beyond the voltage that a sweet
Dessert infuses, or a street musician,
To draw the lightning. Yet her isotope
Perished forever in it. As the waiter
Brings fresh wine, the grim, drowned point breaks water.

Santorini: Stopping the Leak

Not that I've lost or am about to lose
More than on the one hand (or one foot)
An ingrown guest, and on the other, well,
Greece itself. Corrupted whites and blues,
Taverns torn down for banks, the personnel
Grown fat and mulish, marbles clogged with soot . . .
Things just aren't what they were—no more am I,
No more is Nelly. The good word's goodbye

—Or so at least the radiologist's
Black box thought, humming it for all prognosis.
Goodbye. One smelt it as a scorching, read
The heat in shielded eyes and sausage wrists
Throughout his waiting room, where each was fed
Terror and time in exact, equal doses.
As for our meal tonight—which far-out lab
Prepares and serves it: Gemini? the Crab?

We must be light, light-footed, light of soul,
Quick to let go, to tighten by a notch
The broad, star-studded belt Earth wears to feel
Hungers less mortal for a vanished whole.
Light-headed at the last? Our lives unreal
Except as jeweled self-windings, a deathwatch
Of heartless rhetoric I punctuate,
Spitting the damson pit onto the plate?

And if (weeks later, Athens) life still weighs
Too heavily, why, leave the bulk behind.
Give M the bed. Let what was done in it
Parch at a glance from certain killing rays,
And the trunk-oubliette's black yawn admit
Such pictures, records, books as we've consigned,
Poor well-bred things in panic, to the freighter
(Bound for yet more life) Prestidigitator.

On this last evening, once tiny flames
Have danced within my pupils to consume
Letters and photographs, once M, dead drunk,
Muttering of bad faith, though he "names no names",
Has sobered up enough to lift the trunk,
Alone I've stretched out in a rifled room,
Aching for sleep. There comes to me instead
—Brilliantly awake but cased in lead—

A cinéma-mensonge. Long, flowing fits
Of seeing—whose? Utterly not my own:
Bayonet fixed, one olive-skinned Iraqi
Guarding the stairwell of a wartime Ritz;
The look outflashing from his brass and khaki,
That single living cell needed to clone
In depth a double, phantom yet complete
With skills and jokes, cradle to winding-sheet;

His moonbaked slum, muezzin cry and tank
Rumble, the day Grandfather plucked the goose,
The sore in bloom on a pistachio-eyed
Tea-shop girl above the riverbank
—Vignettes as through a jeweler's loupe descried,
Swifter now, churning down the optic sluice,
Faces young, old, to rend the maître d's
Red cord, all random, ravenous images

Avid for inwardness, and none but driven
To gain, like the triumphant sperm, a table
Set for one—wineglass, napkin, and rosebud?
Or failing that, surrender to blue heaven
Its droplet of pure ego, salt as blood?
The warm spate bears me on, helpless, unable
Either to sink or swim, though knowing whence
My trouble springs. Psychic incontinence.

Santorini: Stopping the Leak

A ghost-leak in the footsole. Fighting free
Of sheets that flap off spectral over tiles,
Like bats in negative, sobbing for air
I hobble to the mirror, wordlessly
Frame this petition to its oval, where
Behind a twitching human curtain smiles
Those revels' Queen, in easy ownership,
Sated, my vigor coloring her lip:

I whose demotic commune at your kiss
Took on new senses, snowflake-singular
Facets and symmetries, even as I fall
Back out of mind, yours, anyone's to this
Upsteaming human thaw, babble and brawl
Of now no thought, O that the shattered star,
The music-maker, broadcast limb from limb,
Be made whole, Lady—hear and remember him!

No answer. Or—? In gloom the peevish buzz
Of a wee wingèd one-watt presence short-
Circuiting compulsively the panes
Gone white. *My* drained self doesn't yet . . . yet does!
From some remotest galaxy in the veins
A faint, familiar pulse begins. The wart,
Alive and ticking, that I'd thought destroyed.
No lasting cure? No foothold on the void?

Its tiny secret agent watchful still,
Just where I'd counted on—say an oblivion
That knew its limits. Here was Santorini
Once more, blue deeps, white domes, in imbecile
Symbiosis with the molten genie.
I hear the ferrous, feather-light diluvian
Lava clink at a knife-tap from our guide;
Once more attain, Nelláki at my side—

Grumpy all day because a civil note
Had come by hand, before the morning mail,
Professing the three sisters "desolate"
(One with lumbago, one with a sore throat,
The third with friends in Athens—well, that's Fate)
Not to receive us. So goodbye, roast quail,
French wines and pastries briefer than a bubble . . .
We must be light!—once more attain the double

Site of our last excursion: Prophet Elias'
Radar-crowned monastery, reached by mule.
(Oven, winepress, lentil boutique, and loom.
A sunken door. We rose from hand and knee as
Oil lamps awoke an underground classroom.
Here, throughout centuries of Turkish rule,
Small pupils widening, their abbot set
Before them bread and wine—the Alphabet

Pruned of meaning to dry glottal kernel,
Gaunt root and stock that, quickened, resurrect
Sibyl and scribe's illuminated leaves—
Food for thought even now in this nocturnal
Limbo of straw children, scarecrow sleeves
Lifting their Book of Life mute with neglect,
While overhead a flickering in fetters
Descended on the office of dead letters.)

Behind us then. Next, down and up the gorge,
To gain, past a toy chapel to Saint Michael,
The precinct of Apollo of the Herds
—Of tourists? Not that day. A heavenly forge,
Hammer and tongs, our solitude, our words
Snapped up by North Wind, bellowed to recycle
The bare, thyme-tousled world we'd stumbled on,
Its highbrow wholly given to the Sun

Who beamingly returned the gift. We felt
A stone heart quicken, a deep fault made whole.
Far and wide round us infant waters laughed.
But He meant business also. Having knelt
In amused piety, and photographed
Our Friend, *and* fingered, open-mouthed, the hole
Burnt through my film—by one split-second glance!—
I drew a breath. So much for radiance.

Here, finally, music that would take Satie
Twenty-five hundred years to reinvent
Put naked immaturity through paces
Of a grave dance—as if catastrophe
Could long be lulled by slim waists and shy faces.
Our "worst" in part lived through, part imminent,
We made on sore feet, and by then *were* made,
For a black beach, a tavern in the shade.

AFTER THE BALL

Clasping her magic
Changemaking taffeta
(Old rose to young spinach
And back) I'd taken

Such steps in dream logic
That the Turnstile at Greenwich
Chimed with laughter—
My subway token.

JAMES MERRILL

James Merrill was born in New York City and now lives in Stonington, Connecticut. He is the author of nine books of poems, which have won him two National Book Awards (for *Nights and Days* and *Mirabell*), the Bollingen Prize in Poetry (for *Braving the Elements*) and the Pulitzer Prize (for *Divine Comedies*). *From the First Nine: Poems* 1946–1976, a selection from these, appeared in 1982 with a companion volume, *The Changing Light at Sandover*, which included the long narrative poem begun with "The Book of Ephraim" (from *Divine Comedies*), plus *Mirabell: Books of Number* and *Scripts for the Pageant* in their entirety. The latter received the Book Critics Circle Award in poetry for 1983. He has also written two novels, *The (Diblos) Notebook* (1965) and *The Seraglio* (1957), and two plays, *The Immortal Husband* (first produced in 1955 and published in Playbook the following year), and, in one act, *The Bait*, published in Artist's Theatre (1960).